Duchess's High School

UNION J

THE X FACTOR

Charlie Tink

"Union J have touched my heart & life in many ways since first appearing on the British television show X Factor, this has taken me to a place where writing this must became a must for me."

Charlie Tink

Union J are :

Jamie Hamblett (JJ) 24

George Shelley 19

Josh Cuthbert 20

Jaymi Hensley 22.

From:

JJ – Newmarket

George – Bristol

Josh – Ascot

Jaymi - Luton

Category:

Groups

Mentor:

Louis.

Union J say: "We're four normal down to earth guys who love to sing."

Jaymi, Josh and JJ auditioned for The X Factor as a three piece called Triple J and got through to Bootcamp. After Rough Copy left the show Louis asked them to come back to the competition for Judges Houses and he added 19 year-old George Shelley to the group. They then became Union J.

Jaymi is a part time singing and dancing teacher, Josh works in IT Sales, JJ works with horses and George works part-time in a coffee shop. JJ was a jockey from the age of 15 - following in his dad and brother's footsteps and Josh starred in the West End musical Chitty Chitty Bang Bang when he was 14. His nan Jean spent over £800 on tickets to see him in the show – she went every week! George plays the guitar – he taught himself to play with help from his granddad when he got his first guitar at the age of 13.

Triple J were together for eight months before they auditioned for the show and they got on really well with George at Bootcamp so they are pleased he has joined the group: "We're so happy to be a four piece. The group feels so right together, it feels like we've been together for years!"

The X Factor is a British television music competition to find new singing talent, contested by aspiring singers drawn from public auditions.

Created by Simon Cowell, the show began in September 2004 and has since aired annually from August/September through to December. It is presently (2012) in its ninth series. The show is produced Fremantle Media's Thames and Cowell's production company SYCOtv.

It is broadcast on the ITV network in the United Kingdom and TV3 in Ireland, with spin-off behind-the-scenes show *The Xtra Factor* screened on ITV2. It is the originator of the international *The X Factor* franchise.

The X Factor was devised as a replacement for the highly successful *Pop Idol*, which was put on indefinite hiatus after its second series, largely because Cowell, who was a judge on *Pop Idol*, wished to launch a show to which he owned the television rights.

The perceived similarity between the two shows later became the subject of a legal dispute. The "X Factor" of the title refers to the undefinable "something" that makes for star quality.

The original judging panel was Cowell, Sharon Osbourne and Louis Walsh. Dannii Minogue joined the panel in series 4, and Cheryl Cole replaced Osbourne in series 5 after her departure. After series 7, Cowell and Cole both left to judge the American version of the show whilst Minogue left the show due to commitments on *Australia's Got Talent*.

Kelly Rowland, Tulisa Contostavlos and Gary Barlow then joined Walsh on the judging panel for series 8, though Rowland announced she would not return for series 9 and was replaced by Nicole Scherzinger.

Since 2007, the show has been presented by Dermot O'Leary, who replaced original host Kate Thornton. The show is split into a series of phases, following the contestants from auditions through to the grand finale. In the original televised audition phase of the show, contestants sang in an audition room in front of just the judges.

Fromseries 6 onwards, auditionees sing on a stage in front of the judges and a live audience. Successful auditionees go through to "bootcamp" and then to "judges' houses", where judges narrow down the acts in their category down to three or four acts to mentor for the live shows, where the public vote for their favourite acts following weekly live performances by the contestants.

There have been eight winners to date:

Steve Brookstein, Shayne Ward, Leona Lewis, Leon Jackson, Alexandra Burke, Joe McElderry, Matt Cardle and Little Mix. Winners receive a recording contract with record label Syco Music with a stated value of £1 million. (This includes a cash payment to the winner, but the majority is allocated to marketing and recording costs.

The winning contestant's single from 2004 till 2010 was released in time for the end-of-year chart battle for the UK's Christmas number one, a spot which was gained in 2005, 2006, 2007, 2008 and 2010.

In 2011, the winner's single was released a week earlier. All of the winners' singles have gone on to achieve the number one chart position nevertheless, with Brookstein and McElderry claiming the New Year's number one spot a week later instead, and Little Mix a week earlier. As of September 2012, a total of 29 number-one singles have been released by artists who have appeared on the show.

The show is the biggest television talent competition in Europe and has proved hugely popular with the public. Series 6 attracted 200,000 auditionees and peaked at 19.7 million UK viewers (a 63.2% audience share).

10 million votes were cast in the series 6 final.[6] On 18 October 2010, ITV announced that Cowell had signed a three-year contract renewing *The X Factor* until 2013

The X Factor was created by Sony Music Entertainment A&R judge Simon Cowell as a replacement for *Pop Idol*.

Cowell, who was a judge on *Pop Idol*, wished to launch a show which he owned the rights to. *Pop Idol*'s first series was massively successful, and while the second series was also successful, the viewers figure for its finale dropped.

Some including *Pop Idol* judge Pete Waterman considered Michelle McManus an unworthy winner.

In 2004, ITV announced a new show created by Cowell, with no involvement from *Pop Idol* creator Simon Fuller—*The X Factor*.

For series 1–3 the competition was split into three categories:

16–24s (solo acts aged 16–24), Over 25s (solo acts aged 25 and over) and Groups (including duos).

In series 4–5, the minimum age was lowered to 14, creating a 14–24 age group.

With the addition of a fourth judge in series 4, this was split into separate male and female sections, making four categories in all:

"Boys" (14–25 males)

"Girls" (14–25 females)

Over 25s and Groups.

For series 6, the minimum age returned to 16, meaning that the "Boys" category became 16–25 males and the "Girls" category became 16–25 females. For series 7, the age group boundaries were changed, and the Over 25s became Over 28s, with the Boys and Girls categories becoming 16–28. It was changed back to Over 25s for series 8. For series 9, the category reverted to the Over 28s.

There are five stages to the competition:

- Stage 1: Producers' auditions (these auditions decide who will sing in front of the judges)

- Stage 2: Judges' auditions

- Stage 3: Bootcamp

- Stage 4: Judges' houses

- Stage 5: Live shows (finals)

A round of first auditions is held in front of producers months before the show is aired, either by application and appointment, or at "open" auditions that anyone can attend.

These auditions, held at various venues around the UK, attract very large crowds. The auditions themselves are not televised, but shots of crowds waving and "judges' cars" arriving are filmed and later spliced in with the televised auditions shot later in the year. The production team supply the crowds with "home-made" signs.

After waiting at the venue for hours and filming more inserts of screaming and waving, candidates are given a brief audition by someone from the production team.[11] Should they pass that audition (either for reasons of talent or for the potential of making entertaining television), they are given a "golden ticket" that allows them to sing to a more senior production member.

Only candidates who successfully pass that second and third auditions are invited to perform to the judges.

The televised version misrepresents the process by implying that the entire huge crowds all perform to the judges.

Camera shots take up to 6 hours to record before the auditions are started, with the production team constantly misleading the auditionees.

A selection of the auditions in front of the judges – usually the best, the worst and the most bizarre (described by Louis Walsh as "the good, the bad and the ugly") – are broadcast over the first few weeks of the show.

In the first five series, each act entered the audition room and delivered a stand-up unaccompanied performance of their chosen song to the judges. From series 6 (2009), the judges' auditions have been held in front of a live audience and the acts sing over a backing track.

If a majority of the judges (two in series 1–3, or three from series 4 onwards) say "yes" then the act goes through to the next stage, otherwise they are sent home.

Over 50,000 people auditioned for series 1, around 75,000 for series 2 and around 100,000 for series 3.

The number of applicants for series 4 reached 150,000, 182,000 people auditioned for series 5, and a record 200,000 people applied for series 6.

Series 7 applicants were given the opportunity to apply by uploading a video audition to the Internet.

In series 9, for the first time, applicants can audition online via Facebook.

The show's producers will also be sending a "mobile audition van" to 18 locations throughout the UK and Ireland so they can audition singers who cannot make the arena auditions

The contestants selected at auditions are further refined through a series of performances at "bootcamp", and then at the "judges' houses" (previously "judges' homes"), until a small number eventually progress to the live finals (nine in series 1, twelve from series 2 to 6, and sixteen from series 7).

Louis Walsh revealed in October 2007 that the houses the contestants visit may not actually belong to the judges, but are sometimes rented for the purpose.

During these stages, the producers allocate each of the judges a category to mentor. In early series this allocation took place after completion of the auditions and prior to bootcamp, but from series 4, all four judges work together at the bootcamp stage.

They collectively choose 24 acts (six from each category) for the next round, and only then find out which category they will mentor.

In series 4 and 6, the judges found out which category they would be mentoring at the same time that the contestants found out their mentor, but in series 5 and 7 the contestants did not know who their mentor was until they revealed themselves at the house.

The judges then disband for the "judges' houses" round, where they reduce their six acts to three for the live shows. In series 7 and 8, a total of 32 acts went through to judges' houses, giving each judge eight acts instead of six.

The selected finalists (either 9, 12, 13 or 16 acts) move into shared accommodation to take part in the show. The house accommodates both contestants and TV production staff and footage from the house is often used in spin-off show *The Xtra Factor*.

In 2009 the house, in West Heath Avenue, Golders Green, received significant press coverage when it was mobbed by fans, leading to the police being called. This led to concerns by the neighbours of the 2010 house in Hyver Hill, Mill Hill that it would receive similar attention, with a local farmer worried his land would be damaged, but local businesses were said to be looking forward to increased trade. The 2011 residence, Connaught House in Hertford Heath had cameras installed for filming.

In 2012, the finalists stayed at the Corinthia Hotel in London.

The finals consist of a series of two live shows, the first featuring the contestants' performances and the second revealing the results of the public voting, culminating in one or more acts being eliminated.

Celebrity guest performers also feature regularly.

These live shows are filmed at The Fountain Studios in Wembley, London. In series 1–5, both live shows were broadcast on Saturday nights. In series 6, the results show moved to Sunday nights.

In series 1, nine acts were put through to the live shows, increased to twelve in series 2. From series 7, following the addition of four wildcards, it increased to 16.

The show is primarily concerned with identifying a potential pop star or star group, and singing talent, appearance, personality, stage presence and dance routines are all important elements of the contestants' performances. In the initial live shows, each act performs once in the first show in front of a studio audience and the judges, usually singing over a pre-recorded backing track.

Dancers are also commonly featured. Acts occasionally accompany themselves on guitar or piano.

In the first two series, acts usually chose a cover of a pop standard or contemporary hit.

In series 1, much was made of the idea that each performer/mentor combination was free to present the performance however they wanted, including performer playing live instruments, or the addition of choirs, backing bands, and dancers. From the third series, each live show has had a different theme;

each contestant's song is chosen according to the theme. A celebrity guest connected to the theme is often invited onto the show, and clips are shown of the guest conversing with the contestants at rehearsal.

After each act has performed, the judges comment on their performance. Heated disagreements, usually involving judges defending their contestants against criticism, are a regular feature of the show. Once all the acts have appeared, the phone lines open and the viewing public vote on which act they want to keep.

Once the number of contestants has been reduced to four (series 1 and 3), five (series 2, 4, 5, 6 and 8), or seven (series 7), the format changes. Each act performs twice in the first show, with the public vote opening after the first performance. This continues until only two (series 1 and 3), three (series 2, 4, 5, 6 and 8) or four (series 7) acts remain. These acts go on to appear in the grand final which decides the overall winner by public vote. In past series some of the more memorable failed auditionees from the early rounds have also returned for a special appearance in the final.

Before the results are announced, there are live or pre-recorded performances from one or more invited celebrities, often with performers connected to the week's theme.

From series 6 onwards, the results show begins with a group performance from the remaining contestants. However, the song is pre-recorded and the contestants mime, due to problems with the number of microphones.

The two acts polling the fewest votes are revealed. Both these acts perform again in a "final showdown", and the judges vote on which of the two to send home.

In the first four series the bottom two contestants reprised their earlier song, but from series 5 they were able to pick new songs. In series 3, a twist occurred where the act with the fewest votes was automatically eliminated, and the two with the next fewest votes performed in the "final showdown" as normal. Ties became possible with the introduction of a fourth judge in series 4.

In the event of a tie the result goes to deadlock, and the act who came last in the public vote is sent home. The actual number of votes cast for each act is not revealed, nor even the order; according to a spokesman, "We would never reveal the voting figures during the competition as it could give contestants an unfair advantage and spoil the competition for viewers".

Once the number of contestants has been reduced to four (series 1, 3, 7 and 8) or five (series 2, 4, 5 and 6), the act which polled the fewest votes is automatically eliminated from the competition (the judges do not have a vote; their only role is to comment on the performances).

In series 1, the eliminated acts also reprised one of their songs in the results show after being voted off.

Series 7

Each judge was given a wildcard, allowing them to bring back one rejected act from judges' houses, thus bringing the number of finalists up from twelve to sixteen. Owing to the addition of the wildcards, the first two results were double eliminations.

Series 8

On the first live show, there was no public vote. Instead, each of the judges selected one of their own acts to eliminate.

Series 9

At the end of judges' houses, it was announced that each judge could bring back one further act back as a wildcard. The public then voted for which of the four wildcards would become the thirteenth finalist.

This left one judge with an extra act.

Scherzinger chose Adam Burridge, Contostavlos chose Amy Mottram, Barlow chose Christopher Maloney and Walsh chose Times Red.

The winner was revealed on the first live show as Maloney.

The winner of *The X Factor* is awarded a £1 million recording contract with Syco Music, in association with Sony Music. In series 5, this deal consisted of a £150,000 cash advance with the balance covering the costs of recording and marketing.

Other highly placed contestants may also be offered recording deals, but this is not guaranteed.

In series 1–3, the premise of *The X Factor* was that the winner would be managed in the industry by their mentor on the show.

With Cowell, Osbourne and Walsh as judges/mentors, any of the three would be qualified to do so. Following the appointment of singer Minogue as a judge in series 4, the same principle could not universally apply. In fact, when Minogue won series 4 with Leon Jackson, a new outside manager was appointed.

The X Factor Live Tour is a live show that tours the UK and Ireland in the months following the conclusion of the series. It features an array of finalists and other memorable contestants from the most recent *The X Factor* series and is hosted by Jeff Brazier.

From series 1 to 3, the *X Factor* judges were music executive and TV producer Simon Cowell, and music managers Sharon Osbourne and Louis Walsh. Paula Abdul was a guest judge at the London auditions in series 3.

After series 3, Walsh was dropped from the show, being replaced by American choreographer Brian Friedman who was hired after impressing Cowell on his show *Grease Is the Word*. A fourth judge was also brought in: Australian singer, actress and *Australia's Got Talent* judge Dannii Minogue.

Cowell hired Minogue after viewing tapes of her judging on *Australia's Got Talent*, and because of her 30 years experience as a singer and performer.

However, Friedman was re-assigned the role of creative director because Cowell believed the judging panel was not working and Walsh then resumed his place on the panel, and the series 4 judging lineup was Cowell, Osbourne, Walsh and Minogue.

Minogue became the first female judge to win after her series 4 victory with Leon Jackson.

Speculation surrounded judging lineup changes for series 5, centering on whether Osbourne would return. On 6 June 2008, six days before filming for series 5 was due to begin, ITV confirmed that Osbourne had left the show, and a number of other artists and producers were approached regarding her replacement, including Mel B, Paula Abdul, Sinitta, and former *Pop Idol* judgePete Waterman.

On 10 June, Girls Aloud singer Cheryl Cole was confirmed as Osbourne's replacement.

Osbourne stated that she left *The X Factor* because she did not enjoy working with Minogue.

Despite rumours that Minogue would leave the show after series 5, all four judges from series 5 returned for series 6.

Cole became the first judge to win two series in a row after her victories in series 5 with Alexandra Burke and series 6 with Joe McElderry

Due to Minogue's maternity leave during series 7, a series of guest judges filled in for her at the audition stages before she rejoined the panel in September. The guest judges were Geri Halliwell, Natalie Imbruglia, Katy Perry, Pixie Lott and Nicole Scherzinger.

In July 2010, Cole was diagnosed with malaria towards the end of the auditions. Bootcamp went ahead with Scherzinger as a guest judge.

On 5 May 2011, it was confirmed that Cowell and Cole would not be returning to the judging panel for series 8.

They announced that they were leaving in order to concentrate on theAmerican version of the programme.

On 14 May, it was announced that Minogue would not be returning either. Of her decision, Minogue said "During discussions for me to return [to *The X Factor*] it became clear that unfortunately, this year, *The X Factor* audition dates in the UK clash with the live shows of *Australia's Got Talent* during June and July.

For this reason I am unable to return.

After Cole, Cowell and Minogue announced their leave, a number of celebrities were linked with judging roles, including Frankie Sandford, Noel Gallagher and Alesha Dixon, though Dixon ruled herself out, due to her commitments with *Strictly Come Dancing*,[58] she later joined Cowell's other show *Britain's Got Talent*.

On 30 May, it was confirmed that Gary Barlow, Tulisa Contostavlos and Kelly Rowland would join Walsh for series 8.

On 29 and 30 October, Rowland was unable to travel back from Los Angeles as she had a throat infection, and was unable to judge the live show, so series 5 winner Alexandra Burke took her place.

Barlow, Walsh and Contostavlos returned for series 9. Rowland left due to other commitments.

Geri Halliwell, Leona Lewis, Nicole Scherzinger, Rita Ora, Mel B andAnastacia all filled in as guest judges during the early stages of the competition until a permanent judge was found.

Scherzinger was confirmed as Rowland's replacement, and reappeared on the panel from the Newcastle auditions on a permanent basis.

The first three series of the show were hosted by Kate Thornton. She was replaced from series 4 by Dermot O'Leary who signed a contract worth £1 million to present two series of the programme on ITV.

O'Leary was not forced to leave the *Big Brother* franchise and continued to present *Big Brother* sister shows during summer 2007.

However, O'Leary announced that *Big Brother: Celebrity Hijack* was to be his last *Big Brother* hosting role so he could focus on presenting *The X Factor*.

Brian Friedman continued his role as performance coach and choreographer (billed as "Creative Director") from series 4 until series 7, but left to join with the American version.

Brian Burke and Elizabeth Honan replaced for series 8, although Friedman returned for three weeks in series 9. Yvie Burnett has been *The X Factor*'s vocal coach since series 2, but was replaced in series 7 by Ali Tennant andSavan Kotecha. However, Tennant's contract was ended before the live shows and Burnett was reinstated.

In series 7, Richard "Biff" Stannard started work as show song producer for Minogue's contestants, and Grace Woodward joined the series as Fashion Director.

Voice-overs are provided by Peter Dickson and Enn Reitel.

Viewing figures of around 10 million were claimed for series 2 and 4, and 11 to 12 million for series 5. Over three million public votes were cast in series 2 and six million in the first part of the final. The series 3 final attracted eight million votes and a peak of 12.6 million viewers.

The series 4 final drew 12.7 million viewers – a 55% share of the terrestrial TV audience.

In series 5, 12.8 million tuned in to see the 29 November 2008 show featuring guest Britney Spears, a new *X Factor* record.

The series 5 final peaked with 14.6 million viewers.

The series 6 final was watched by 19.1 million viewers (a 63.2% audience share) with 10 million votes cast[6] and the series 7 final topped this attracting 19.4 million viewers with over 15 million votes cast but the series 8 final was a large drop from this, with 13.456 million viewers.

The BBC's rival talent show *Strictly Come Dancing* initially beat *The X Factor* in viewing figures in 2004, although in recent years *The X Factor* has reversed this trend, and when the shows went head-to-head for the first time *The X Factor* attracted a larger audience share.

It rates as ITV's most popular programme whilst it is broadcast, and is the first format (along with *Britain's Got Talent*) in years to knock *Coronation Street* off the top.

At the 2005 British Comedy Awards, *The X Factor* beat *Friday Night with Jonathan Ross* and *Ant & Dec's Saturday Night Takeaway* to take the award for Best Comedy Entertainment Programme, prompting Simon Cowell to remark "We're not a comedy programme, we're a serious factual drama".

In both 2005 and 2006, *The X Factor* won the award for "Most Popular Entertainment Programme" at the National Television AwardsAt the same awards in 2007, the show also won the award for "Most Popular Talent Show".

In 2008 it lost out to *Strictly Come Dancing* at the TV Quick Awards, TRIC Awards and National Television Awards, despite beating it in the ratings In 2009, *The X Factor* won "Best Talent Show" at the National Television Awards.

The show won the Entertainment award at the 2010 Royal Television Society Awards, described as "Undeniably a brilliant, genre-defining piece of television; the team behind this show never rest on their laurels and are determined to continually raise the bar and set new standards. Must-see television, which everyone talks about on a Monday morning.

At the 2011 National Television Awards, *The X Factor* won the Talent Show award, beating *Strictly Come Dancing*, *Britain's Got Talent* and *Dancing on Ice*. At the 2012 National Television Awards, *The X Factor* again beat *Strictly Come*

Dancing, Britain's *Got Talent* and *Dancing on Ice* to the award. The show also won Best UK TV Show at the 2012 Kids' Choice Awards

The X Factor has, from the outset, attracted criticism. Recurring allegations are: that the excessive commercialism of the show detracts from of its supposed purpose of unearthing musical talent and even actively damages and distorts the UK music industry; that auditionees at mass auditions are shabbily treated; that controversy is deliberately courted and orchestrated, and supposedly spontaneous scenes are staged and scripted; that problems with phone lines leave members of the public unable to vote for their favourite acts; and that contestants are manipulated and unfairly edited.

This criticism became very public in 2009 when a Facebook campaign targeted against *The X Factor* and its effect on British music took "Killing in the Name" by Rage Against the Machine to the Christmas number one spot at the expense of the *X Factor* winner's single by Joe McElderry.

In 2009, *The X Factor* received heavy criticism when contestant Toby Barnes was booted off of the show after reaching judges' houses.

His mentor, Simon Cowell, was forced to let him go after it was revealed that he already had a record deal and was signed to Universal Music and Polydor Records

The Xtra Factor is a companion show that is broadcast on digital channel ITV2 and on TV3 Ireland on Saturday and Sunday nights after the main ITV show.

It features behind-the-scenes footage of *The X Factor* and shows the emotional responses of the contestants after the judges comment on their performances. The commissioning of *The Xtra Factor* was prompted by the success of *Big Brother's Little Brother*, a *Big Brother* companion show screened on E4.

The Xtra Factor features extra auditions, bootcamp performances and judges' houses performances and behind-the-scenes footage.

In past series, there have been competitions and games featuring the judges and presenters. During the live shows the programme feature behind-the-scenes footage and answers live video and phone calls for the judges and contestants.

Facebook statuses and Tweets are read out as well. It also shows the emotional responses of the contestants after the judges comment on their performances. A celebrity panel is usually featured, who give their opinions on the contestants.

Until series 3, *The Xtra Factor* was hosted by Ben Shephard. The voiceover on series 1 to 6 was Peter Dickson. Shephard did not return for series 4 after being upset at not getting the main ITV presenting job, and Fearne Cotton took over as host, for series 4 only, before leaving the show to concentrate on her career in America.

Allegations of a falling-out with Simon Cowell were also reported. For series 5, Cotton was replaced by presenter and close friend Holly Willoughby.

Willoughby first presented *The Xtra Factor* on 9 August 2008, a week before series 5 was broadcast. Konnie Huq replaced Willoughby as the new *Xtra Factor* presenter for series 7.

However, Huq decided to depart from the series in March 2011 because of work commitments.

On 31 May 2011, Caroline Flack and Olly Murs were confirmed as the new co-hosts for series 8 by *The X Factor*'s official Twitter page.

Cameras follow the finalists during their day, and in early series some of the footage was aired in a spin-off show called ***The Xtra Factor: The Aftermath***, which was broadcast in the middle of the week on ITV2.

The Xtra Factor: Xcess All Areas was a live show in which there were interviews, games and trips around the contestants' homes. The show also let viewers know which songs the contestants would be singing in the next live show. Both shows were axed after series 3 due to ITV2 cutting back on spin-off programing.

Each year after the series has come to an end, *The Xtra Factor* has a week of special programmes titled *Best and Worst*, featuring the best and worst auditions from the previous series, ranging from two to five episodes each year.

A 60-minute special titled **The Winner's Story** is broadcast each year over the festive period, featuring the winner of that year's *X Factor*. Cameras follow the winner from the announcement of the result through the lead-up to the Christmas number one.

As from 2010, one week before each series due to start, there features a special called **X Factor Rewind** looking back at the previous year's contestants and what happened to them during *The X Factor* and what has happened to them since the show ended.

The X Factor: Battle of the Stars was a celebrity special edition of *The X Factor*, which screened on ITV, starting on 29 May 2006 and lasting for eight consecutive nights.

Pop Idol was intended to be broadcast in its place as *Celebrity Pop Idol* but was stopped shortly before transmission, when ITV selected *The X Factor* instead.

Nine celebrity acts participated, singing live in front of the nation and facing the judges of the previous *The X Factor* series, Simon Cowell, Sharon Osbourne and Louis Walsh. Voting revenues were donated to the celebrities' chosen charities.

The contestants were Michelle Marsh, Nikki Sanderson, Matt Stevens, Lucy Benjamin, Gillian McKeith, Chris Moyles, Paul Daniels and Debbie McGee, James Hewitt and Rebecca Loos, and "The Chefs", a quartet of celebrity chefs comprising Jean-Christophe Novelli, Aldo Zilli, Paul Rankin and Ross Burden.

The winner of the show was Lucy Benjamin, mentored by Walsh.

It was reported on 26 August 2006 that Simon Cowell had decided not to do a second edition, describing it as "pointless" and adding "we are never going to do it again"

As of December 2011, the show has spawned eight number-one winners' singles (five of which have been the Christmas number one), four number-one charity singles, and a total of 15 number-one singles by contestants who have appeared on the show (including winners and runners-up).

By series 6 (2009) it had seemingly become such a certainty that the *X Factor* winner would gain the Christmas number one slot every year that bookmakers William Hill were considering withdrawing from the 30-year tradition of betting on the outcome.

However, hostility to the show's stranglehold on the Christmas number one slot from some quarters had prompted attempts to propel an alternative song to the 2008 Christmas number one spot, and in 2009 a similar internet-led campaign was successful, taking Rage Against the Machine's "Killing in the Name" to Christmas number one at the expense of *The X Factor* winner Joe McElderry.

McElderry's single climbed to the top of the chart a week later.

In series 1–2, the winner's debut album would be released a few months after their victory in the show. The album would contain some new material but would consist largely of cover versions.

This format changed with series 3 winnerLeona Lewis. Cowell, Lewis's *X Factor* mentor and newly-appointed manager, said: "We could have gone into the studio for a month, made the record quick, and thrown it out. It would have been the wrong thing to do."

The success of Lewis's debut album *Spirit* ensured that the debut albums of future series winners (such as series 4 winner Leon Jackson) would consist more of new material than of cover versions

During the fifth series of the show, the finalists released *Hero* in aid of Help for Heroes which reached number one in the UK singles charts. Following the success of the song, Cowell has announced that a charity single will be released annually.

He is quoted as saying: "Following last year's record we made with the *X Factor* finalists in aid of Help For Heroes, we decided we wanted to do something annually on the show to help good causes."

The 2009 single was a cover of the Michael Jackson song *You Are Not Alone* which was released in aid of Great Ormond Street Hospital and reached number one.

The 2010 single was a cover of David Bowie's Heroes, with proceeds once again going to the Help for Heroes charity. In 2011, the finalists released "Wishing on a Star" by Rose Royce and the proceeds were donated to Together for Short Lives.

This song features previous contestants JLS and One Direction

Merchandise

DVDs

- Series 1: *The X Factor Revealed: The Greatest Auditions Ever* (2005)
- Series 2: *The X Factor: The Greatest Auditions Ever* (2006)
- Series 3: *The X Factor Revealed* (2007)

Games

- Series 4: *The X Factor* – interactive DVD game (2007)
- Series 4: *The X Factor Sing* – karaoke console game (2007)
- Series 5: *The X Factor: The Board Game* (2009)
- Series 5: *Top Trumps X Factor* – card game (2008)
- Series 7: *The X Factor* – karaoke console game (2010)

Books

- Series 1–3: *The X Factor: Access All Areas* (2007)
- Series 6: *The X Factor Annual* (2009)[117]
- Series 7: *The X Factor Annual* (2010)
- Series 7: *The Xtra Factor Annual* (2010)[118]
- Series 8: *The X Factor Annual* (2011)

Magazines

- *X Magazine* – weekly publication starting in 2010

Printed in Great Britain
by Amazon.co.uk, Ltd.,
Marston Gate.